Robert Lowry

Glad Refrain for the Sunday School

A new collection of songs for worship

Robert Lowry

Glad Refrain for the Sunday School
A new collection of songs for worship

ISBN/EAN: 9783337038243

Printed in Europe, USA, Canada, Australia, Japan

Cover: Foto ©Lupo / pixelio.de

More available books at **www.hansebooks.com**

The Glad Refrain

for

The Sunday School.

A NEW COLLECTION OF

SONGS FOR WORSHIP.

Edited by

ROBERT LOWRY and W. HOWARD DOANE.

BOTH YOUNG MEN, AND MAIDENS; OLD MEN, AND CHILDREN: LET THEM PRAISE THE NAME OF THE LORD.—Ps. cxlviii., 12, 13.

Published in Separate Editions of Round and Character Notes.

BIGLOW & MAIN,
76 East Ninth Street, New York. | 81 Randolph Street, Chicago.

MAY BE ORDERED THROUGH BOOKSELLERS AND MUSIC DEALERS

COPYRIGHT 1886, BY BIGLOW & MAIN.

SALUTATION.

Glad Refrain is in the line of the successful books edited by the same authors.

Glad Refrain takes up the old Gospel theme—CHRIST in His character and His work.

Glad Refrain is intended for practical use in the Song Service of the Sunday School.

Glad Refrain includes hymns both for the young and for grown-up people.

Glad Refrain presents music such as Sunday Schools delight to sing.

Glad Refrain is projected on a grade that recognizes an improved taste in the material for the Service of Song.

Glad Refrain does not contain any music that has the soul taken out of it by excess of technical polishing.

THE EDITORS.

For the convenience of Superintendents who desire a schedule for the Sunday School Session, we suggest the following:

Time—2:30.	Reading Lesson.	Announcements.
Bell Tap.	Singing.	Blackboard Exercise.
Silence.	Time—2:55.	Miscellaneous.
Singing.	Studying Lesson.	Closing Service.
Opening Service.	Time—3:30.	Singing.
Prayer.	Bell Tap.	Time—3:50.
Singing.	Perfect Order.	Dismission.

If another hour is used, the same intervals will be found desirable.

SCRIPTURE SELECTIONS.

1. The Lord's Prayer.

Our Father who art in heaven,
Hallowed be thy name.
Thy kingdom come.
Thy will be done on earth, as it is in heaven.
Give us this day our daily bread:
And forgive us our debts, as we forgive our debtors.
And lead us not into temptation, but deliver us from evil:
For thine is the kingdom, and the power, and the glory, for ever.
Amen.

2. Opening Service.

SUPERINTENDENT.—The law of the LORD is perfect, converting the soul:
School.—The testimony of the LORD is sure, making wise the simple:
SUPT.—The statutes of the LORD are right, rejoicing the heart:
School.—The commandment of the LORD is pure, enlightening the eyes:
SUPT.—The fear of the LORD is clean, enduring for ever:
School.—The judgments of the LORD are true and righteous altogether.
SUPT.—More to be desired are they than gold, yea, than much fine gold;
School.—Sweeter also than honey and the honeycomb.
SUPT.—Moreover, by them is thy servant warned:
School.—And in keeping of them there is great reward.
SUPT.—Let the words of my mouth, and the meditation of my heart, be acceptable in thy sight,
School.—O LORD, my strength and my redeemer.

3. Opening Service.

SUPT.—O come let us sing unto the Lord; let us make a joyful noise to the Rock of our salvation.
School.—Let us come before his presence with thanksgiving, and make a joyful noise unto him with psalms.
SUPT.—They that wait upon the Lord shall renew their strength; they shall mount up with wings as eagles;
School.—They shall run, and not be weary; they shall walk, and not faint.
SUPT.—It is a good thing to give thanks unto the Lord.
School.—Unto thee, O God, do we give thanks; for that thy name is near thy wondrous works declare.
SUPT.—Let thy mercy, O Lord, be upon us, according as we hope in thee.
School.—O Lord of hosts, blessed is the man that trusteth in thee.
SUPT.—Deal bountifully with thy servant, that I may keep thy word.
School.—Open thou mine eyes, that I may behold wondrous things out of thy law.
SUPT.—Quicken thou me according to thy word.
School.—Make me to understand the way of thy precepts.
SUPT.—Teach me, O LORD, the way of thy statutes, and I shall keep it unto the end.
School.—Give me understanding, and I shall keep thy law; yea, I shall observe it with my whole heart.

4. Responsive Service.

SUPT.—Blessed are the poor in spirit: for theirs is the kingdom of heaven.
School.—Blessed are they that mourn: for they shall be comforted.
SUPT.—Blessed are the meek: for they shall inherit the earth.
School.—Blessed are they which do hunger and thirst after righteousness: for they shall be filled.
SUPT.—Blessed are the merciful: for they shall obtain mercy.
School.—Blessed are the pure in heart: for they shall see God.
SUPT.—Blessed are the peacemakers: for they shall be called the children of God.
School.—Blessed are they which are persecuted for righteousness' sake: for theirs is the kingdom of heaven.
SUPT.—Blessed are ye, when men shall revile you, and persecute you, and shall say all manner of evil against you falsely, for my sake.
School.—Rejoice, and be exceeding glad: for great is your reward in heaven: for so persecuted they the prophets which were before you.

5. Missionary Service.

SUPT.—Let the people praise thee, O God; let all the people praise thee.
School.—O let the nations be glad, and sing for joy: for thou shalt judge the people righteously, and govern the nations upon earth.
SUPT.—Let the people praise thee, O God; let all the people praise thee.
School.—Then shall the earth yield her increase; and God, even our God, shall bless us.
SUPT.—God shall bless us, and all the ends of the earth shall fear him.
School.—Let the heavens be glad, and let the earth rejoice: and let men say among the nations, The LORD reigneth.
SUPT.—Behold my servant, whom I uphold, mine elect, in whom my soul delighteth; he shall bring forth judgment to the Gentiles.
School.—He shall not fail nor be discouraged, till he have set judgment in the earth: and the isles shall wait for his law.
SUPT.—God hath made of one blood all nations of men, to dwell on all the face of the earth.
School.—Whosoever shall call on the name of the LORD, shall be saved.

6. Closing Service.

SUPT.—Now unto the King eternal, immortal, invisible, the only wise God, be honor and glory for ever and ever.
School.—Blessed are all they that put their trust in him.
SUPT.—Thy word is a lamp unto my feet, and a light unto my path.
School.—Thou art my hiding place and my shield: I hope in thy word.
SUPT.—Thou makest the outgoings of the morning and evening to rejoice.
School.—At evening time it shall be light.
SUPT.—The Lord watch between me and thee, when we are absent one from another.
School.—He that keepeth Israel shall neither slumber nor sleep.

7. Closing Service.

SUPT.—All scripture is given by inspiration of God, and is profitable for doctrine, for reproof, for correction, for instruction in righteousness.
School.—Blessed are they that hear the word of God, and keep it.
SUPT.—Let the word of Christ dwell in you richly in all wisdom.
School.—Thy word have I hid in mine heart, that I might not sin against thee.
SUPT.—From the rising of the sun, unto the going down of the same, the LORD's name is to be praised.
School.—Unto thee shall the vow be performed.
SUPT.—Grace be to you, and peace, from God our Father, and the Lord Jesus Christ.
School.—The Lord bless thee, and keep thee.

Wait on the Lord. Concluded.

mag - ni - fy His grace, For ev - - - er - - - more.
ev - er, ev - er - more.

No. 3. Hold up the Cross.

Miss F. G. BROWNING. ROBERT LOWRY.

1. By the cross of Christ I lin - ger, Reading there the sto - ry old,
2. By the cross I'm lift - ed near - er To the heart of Him who died;
3. By the cross of Christ my longing For a crown is sat - is - fied;

Traced in blood by God's own fin - ger, When His love to man was told.
Dai - ly grows my vis - ion clear - er To be - hold the Cru - ci - fied.
Thoughts of joy be-yond are thronging, As I stand the cross be - side.

REFRAIN.
Hold up the cross to a dy - ing world, Hold up the cross, hold up the cross;

Hold up the cross to a dy - ing world, Hold up the cross.

Copyright, 1886, by Biglow & Main. (7)

Come at the Call. Concluded.

Wan - der not in dark - ness, broth- er,— walk in the light;
Sweet - ly He is say - ing, broth- er,—"Come un - to me;"
Then at last in glo - ry, broth- er,— joy shall be thine;

There is Truth to guide you, brother,—shining clear and bright. If you heed the
There is Grace to save you, brother,—grace to set you free, If you heed the
There is Love to keep you, brother,—love that is di-vine, If you heed the

Spir - it's voice, and come at the call.
Spir - it's voice, and come at the call. } O come at the
Spir - it's voice, and come at the call.

Come at the call,

call, The Spir-it and the Bride say, Come; O

Come at the call, O come!

come at the call, To our heav'nly Father's home.

Come at the call, Come at the call,

Copyright, 1886, by Biglow & Main.

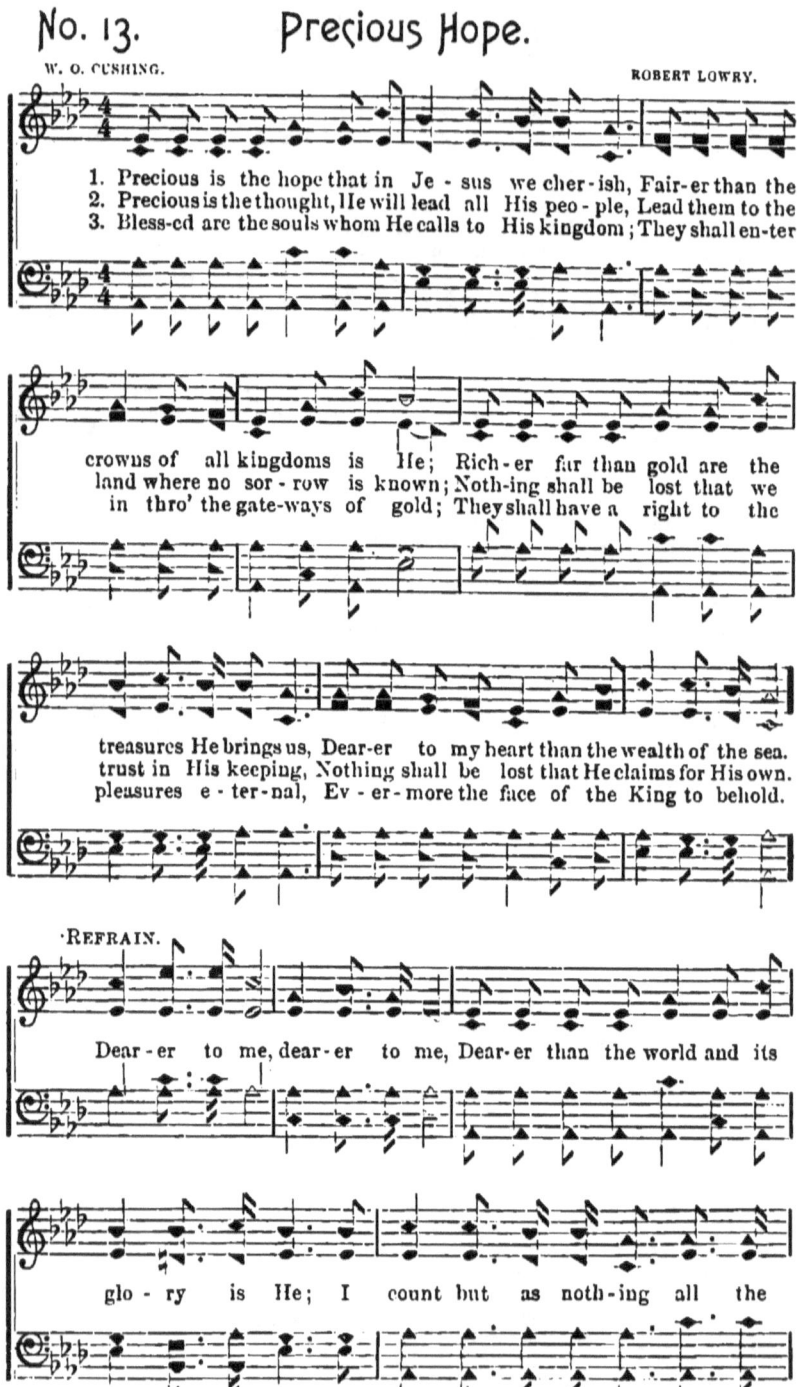

Precious Hope. Concluded.

wealth of the sea, Compared with the joy He has purchased for me.

Copyright, 1886, by Biglow & Main.

No. 14. Daily, Hourly, Lead Me.

Mrs. HARRIET JONES.   W. H. DOANE.

1. Lov-ing Saviour, lead me Ev-ery day and hour; Keep me ev-er
2. O Thou gracious Giv-er, Hear my ear-nest plea; Keep, O keep me
3. Thro' the pathway drear-y Guide me day by day; When oppressed and

near Thee, Hold me by Thy power; Ev-ery moment, Lord, I need Thee;
ev-er Ver-y close to Thee; Let Thy pres-ence ev-er cheer me;
wea-ry, Be my help and stay; In the hour of death, O hide me;

REFRAIN.

O my Sav-iour, lead me.
Keep, O keep me near Thee. } Dai-ly, hour-ly, lead me; Loving Saviour,
Thro' its shad-ow guide me.

lead me; Ev-ery moment lead me, Till I rest with Thee.

Copyright, 1886, by Biglow & Main.   (17)

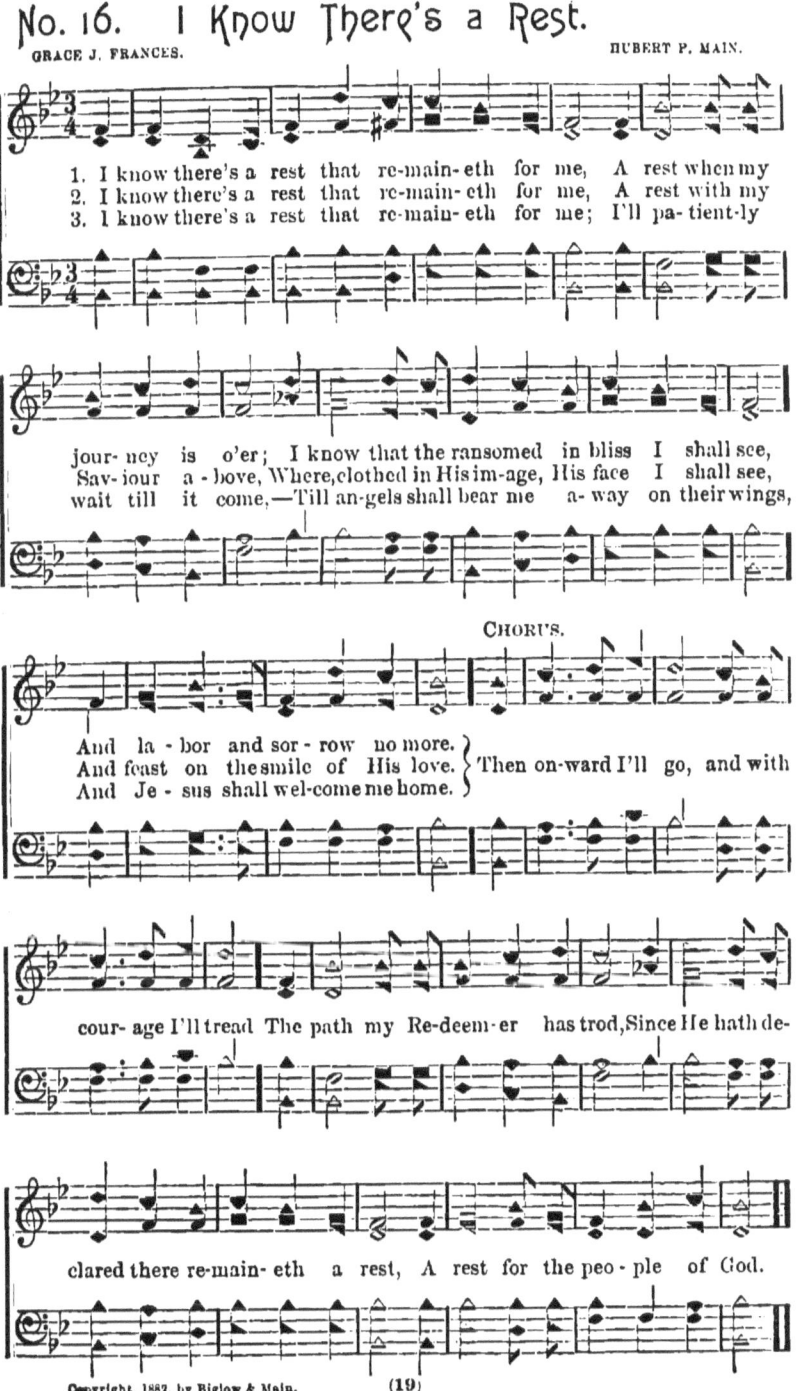

What A Gath'ring That Will Be! Concluded.

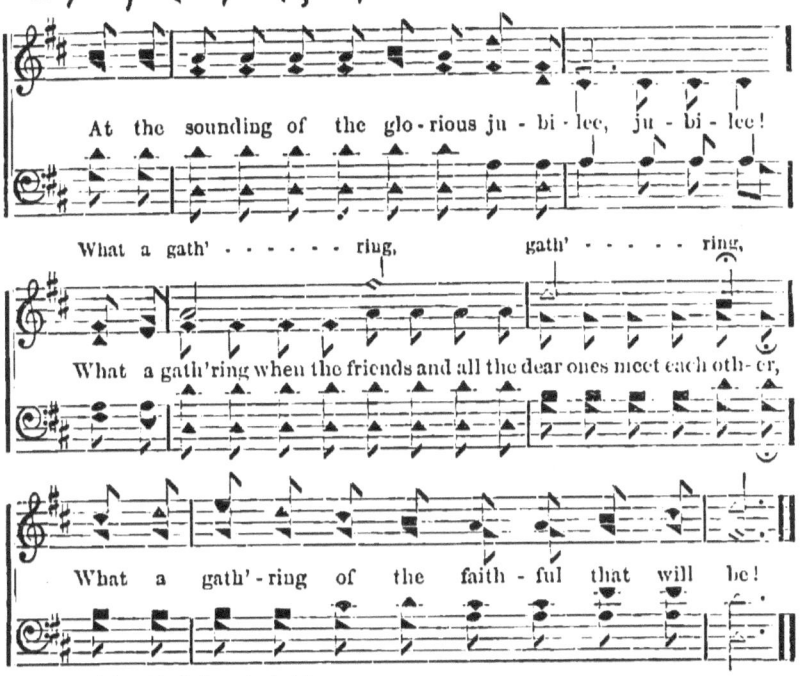

By permission of J. H. Kurzenknabe & Sons.

No. 18. Come, Holy Spirit.

Rev. F. H. MAGOUN. ROBERT LOWRY.

1. Come, Ho-ly Spir-it, Light Divine, Illume this darkened heart of mine;
2. Come, Ho-ly Spir-it, Guide Divine, To this bewildered heart of mine;
3. Come, Ho-ly Com-fort-er Divine, En-ter this troubled heart of mine;
4. Come, Ho-ly Spirit, Strength Divine, In-to this wea-ry heart of mine;

Dis-pel the clouds of doubt and grief, Let Thy bright presence bring relief.
Then shall I nev-er go a-stray From God's own true and holy way.
Then, with Thy gracious presence blest, I shall be filled with sweetest rest.
With en-er-gy my be-ing fill, And make me strong to do God's will.

Copyright, 1886, by Biglow & Main.

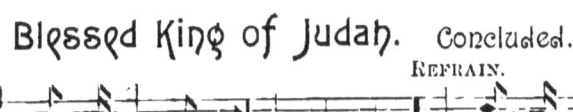

Blessed King of Judah. Concluded.

Copyright, 1886, by Biglow & Main.

No. 22. Benediction.

2 Cor. 13: 14.
Moderato.
ROBERT LOWRY.

Copyright, 1886, by Biglow & Main.

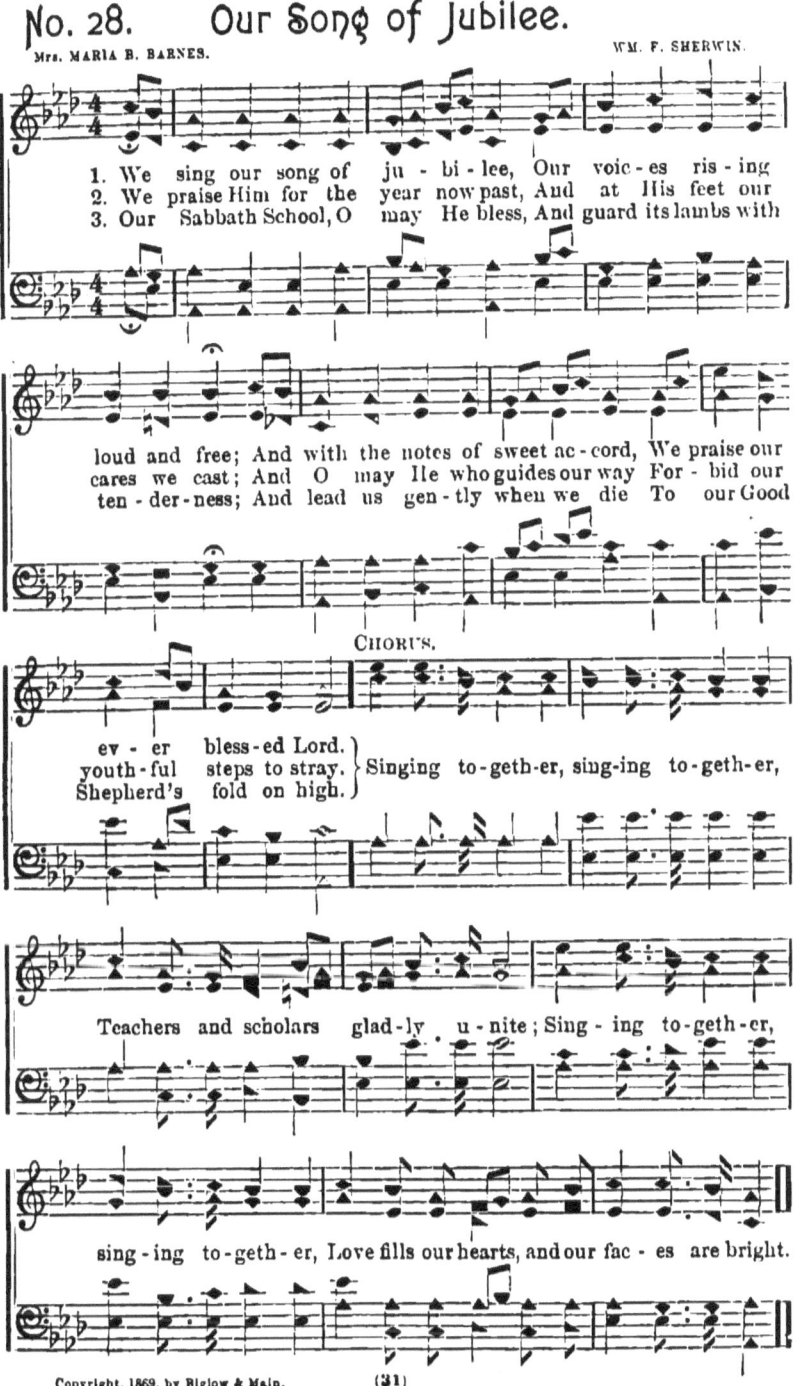

No. 30. Look to the Precious Jesus.

T. P. W.
THOS. P. WESTENDORF.

1. Look to the precious Je - sus, Think of the life He gave; Look to the precious Je - sus, He has the pow'r to save; Wild-ly the waves are dashing, Storm-clouds are hanging near, While lightnings sharp are flashing, Fill-ing the soul with fear.
2. Look to the precious Je - sus, Ask Him for help to - day; Look to the precious Je - sus, Ask Him to lead the way; Safe thro' the clouds of sor - row, Safe o'er the dark'ning tide, In - to the glad to - mor - row, Up to the Father's side.
3. Look to the precious Je - sus, Glad-ly He'll come to thee; Look to the precious Je - sus, Ask Him to make you free; Free from the pow'rs that bind thee, Free from the ways of sin, Free from the thoughts that blind thee, Help-ing a crown to win.

REFRAIN.

Look to the precious Je - sus, Think of the life He gave; Look to the precious Je - sus, He has the pow'r to save.

From "Helping Hand," by per. G. D. Newhall Co.

No. 35. Seek Salvation To-Day.

JOSEPHINE POLLARD.   WM. B. BRADBURY.

1. We nev-er shall be hap-py if we walk the ways of sin,
2. We'll nev-er get to heav-en if we do not learn the way,
3. The tempt-er may as-sail us, but with Je-sus by our side,

'Tis a path that leads on-ward to sor-row; If the right we would pur-
And pre-pare for the jour-ney be-fore us; If for Je-sus we would
And a hope in His pow-er pos-sess-ing, We will make His ho-ly

sue, it is time we should begin, For why need we wait till to-
live, we must always watch and pray, And thus will His ban-ner be
word still our coun-sel and our guide, And count ev-ery tri-al a

CHORUS.

mor-row?
o'er us. } Let us seek sal-va-tion to-day, yes, to-day,
bless-ing.

Seek sal-va-tion to-day; If the crown we would se-cure,

Copyrighted 1867, by W. B. BRADBURY.

Seek Salvation To-Day. Concluded.

We must make our call-ing sure, And seek sal - va - tion to - day.

No. 36. O What a Saviour is Mine.

FANNY J. CROSBY.   ALEX. VAN ALSTYNE.

1. O what a Sav-iour is mine, Lov-ing and ten - der;
2. O what a thrill of de-light Wakes ev-ery feel - ing!
3. Now I can sing of His love; Won-der-ful sto - ry!

All for His glo - ry di - vine Now I sur - ren - der;
Pleas- ure un - earth - ly and bright O - ver me steal - ing;
Now is my treas- ure a - bove, His be the glo - ry;

Trust - ing I came, Plead-ing His name, Then, my trans-
Cleansed from my sin, Hap - py with - in, Mer - cy and
Safe on His breast, Calm-ly I rest; O that my

gres- sion con - fess - ing, Rich was the gift of His bless - ing.
par - don re - ceiv - ing, Great is my peace in be - liev - ing.
soul may for - ev - er Drink of the life - giv - ing riv - er.

Copyright, 1874, by Biglow & Main.

No. 38. Come, Learn of the Meek and Lowly.

GRACE J. FRANCES. HUBERT P. MAIN.

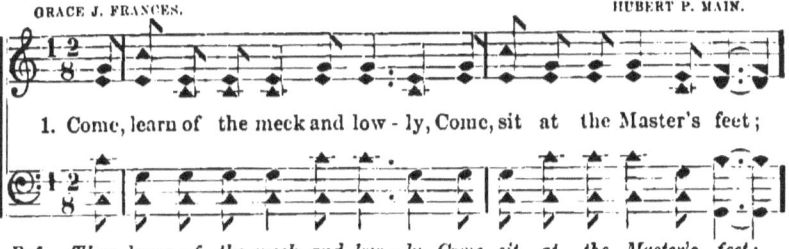

1. Come, learn of the meek and low-ly, Come, sit at the Master's feet;

Ref.—Then learn of the meek and low-ly, Come, sit at the Master's feet;

No place in the world so ho-ly, No place in the world so sweet;

No place in the world so ho-ly, No place in the world so sweet.

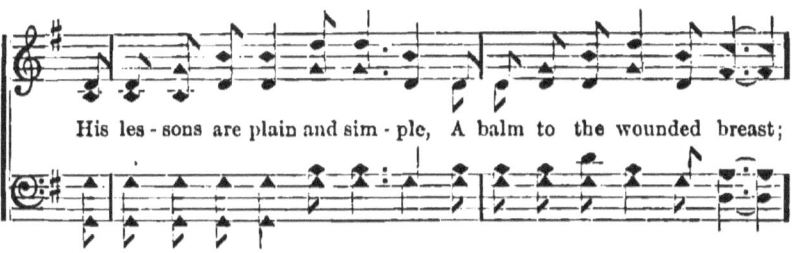

His les-sons are plain and sim-ple, A balm to the wounded breast;

D.C. for Refrain.

He mak-eth our bur-den light-er, And giv-eth His chil-dren rest.

Copyright, 1882, by Biglow & Main.

2 O if we were more like Jesus,
And more from the world apart,
Communing with Him in spirit,
And nearer to Him in heart,—
We should not complain so sadly,
When trouble and care we meet,
But carry at once our sorrows,
And lay them at Jesus' feet.—*Ref.*

3 He wept o'er the holy city,
He wept o'er a loved one dead;
He knoweth our every trial,
And seeth the tears we shed;
O live that our souls may enter
His kingdom with joy complete;
And there, through eternal ages,
We'll sit at the Master's feet.—*Ref.*

Zion's Happy Soldiers. Concluded.

On - - ward, Ev- er true and faith - ful, trust - ing the Lord.

trust-ing in the Lord;

No. 42. Looking Up.

E. M. J.   ROBERT LOWRY.

1. Keep look-ing up, keep look-ing up, The mists will clear a-way; In God's own time His lov-ing hand Will brighten up the day.
2. Keep look-ing up, keep look-ing up, Th' e-ter-nal hills are there; Far, far be-yond these gloomy clouds Are treasures rich and rare.
3. Keep look-ing up, keep look-ing up, With Faith's as-pir-ing eye; The prom-ise is that help will come From Him who dwells on high.
4. Lift up thine eyes, lift up thine eyes, And take the outstretched hand; 'Tis Je-sus bids thee struggle on, And vic-tor thou shalt stand.

REFRAIN.

Keep look-ing up, keep looking up, The mists will clear a - way; In God's own time His lov - ing hand Will brighten all the day.

Copyright, 1886, by Biglow & Main.   (45)

No. 43. All Hail, Blessed Morning.

FANNY J. CROSBY. THEO. F. SEWARD.

1. All hail, blessed morning, With sunshine adorning The world that lay
2. No more shall He languish, Or suf-fer the an-guish He bore on the
3. He liv-eth vic-to-rious, He liv-eth all glo-rious, Thro' Him shall the
4. Then while we a-dore Him, And gather be-fore Him, Our hearts and our

weep-ing o'er Him that was slain; Thou com-est with glad-ness, Dis-
cross when His life blood was shed; Lo! an-gels in won-der, The
cap-tive from bondage be free; The vol-ume of a-ges Pro-
voi-ces u-nit-ed shall praise The great In-ter-ces-sor For

pel-ling our sadness, Thou bringest good tidings, He liv-eth a-gain.
grave rent a-sun-der, Be-held when their Monarch a-rose from the dead.
claims on its pag-es, For-ev-er es-tablished His kingdom shall be.
ev-ery transgressor, The Son of the Highest, the An-cient of days.

CHORUS.
Our Rock is se-cure, Our anch-or is sure, The Lord our Re-
deem-er is might-y to save; Go, her-alds of glo-ry, And

Copyright, 1883, by Biglow & Main.

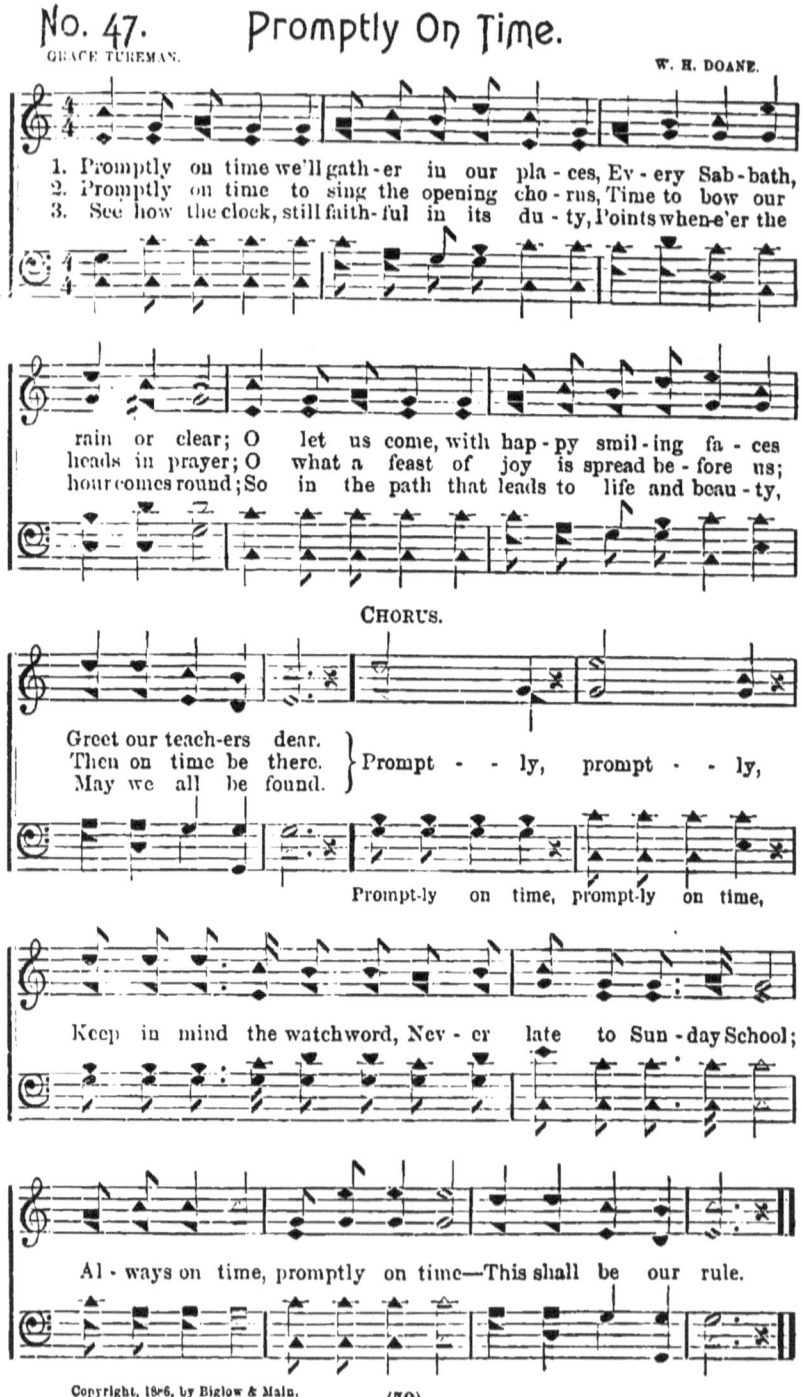

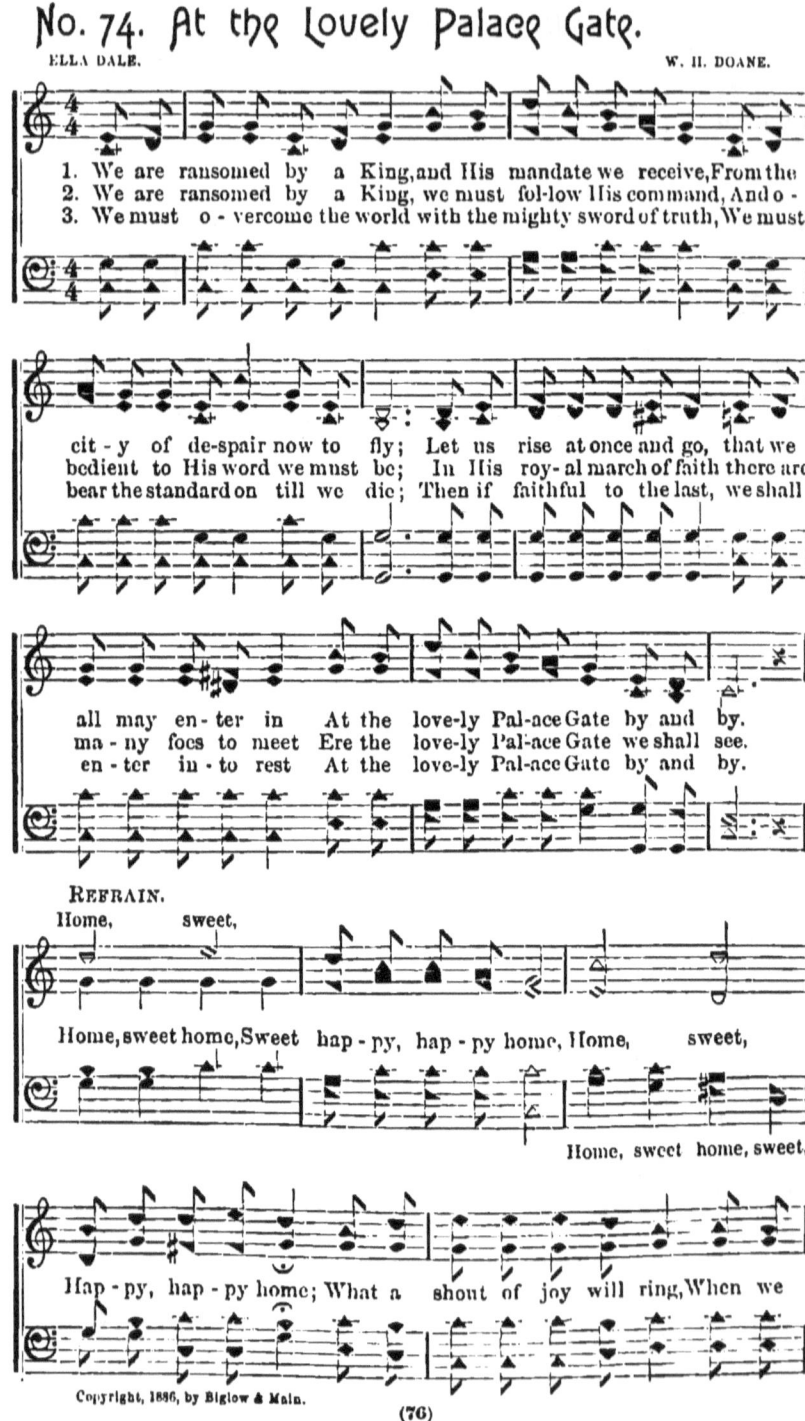

No. 76. Cleansed and Redeemed.

FANNY J. CROSBY.   W. H. DOANE.

1. Cleansed in the blood that was shed on the tree, When Jesus gave Himself as a ransom for me; Cleansed and redeemed in the blood of the Lamb, O glory be to Him that I am what I am.

2. Cleansed and redeemed, this assurance of mine Is witnessed in my heart by His Spirit Divine; Sealed by His grace, now through faith I receive The blessing He bestows on the souls that believe.

D.S.—Cleansed and redeemed in the blood of the Lamb, O glory be to Him that I am what I am.

REFRAIN.

Cleansed and redeemed, yes, cleansed and redeemed, I am happy in my Saviour now;

Copyright, 1886, by Biglow & Main.

3 Cleansed in His blood that from sin can restore,
  I give myself away to be His evermore;
  Cleansed and redeemed, I rejoice while I sing,
  O glory be to Him, my Redeemer and King.—*Ref.*

4 Cleansed and redeemed—O the depth of His love,
  To care for such as I and His mercy to prove;
  Cleansed and redeemed, let my song ever be,
  O glory be to Him for His mercy to me.—*Ref.*

No. 80. Go Lead Them To-Day.

F. J. C. W. H. DOANE.

1. O pit-y the err-ing; How lit-tle we know Their moments of an-guish, Their burden of woe; O think of them kind-ly; God's creatures are they; To Him, their Redeemer, Go lead them to-day.
2. From those who have wandered Why turn we a-side? There's hope for the err-ing, Since Jesus has died; Go lift up the fall-en; God's message o-bey; To Him who will save them, Go lead them to-day.
3. O res-cue the err-ing From sin and de-spair; They need our pro-tec-tion, Our kindness and care; Go plead with them gen-tly; God's lost ones are they; Go bring them to Jesus, Go lead them to-day.

REFRAIN.

Lone-ly, friendless, for-sak-en, Yet the Saviour will hear them; He is waiting to help them, He pit-ies them now.

Copyright, 1886, by Biglow & Main.

No. 84. Our Jubilee Song.

Mrs. E. S. PRENTISS.   W. H. DOANE.

1. Hark, hark the song, glid-ing a-long, Borne on the summer breeze,
2. Green, shad-y bow'rs, sweet, blushing flow'rs, Come with the summer time,
3. Hark, hark the song, float-ing a-long, Borne to the sun-ny land,

far, far a-way; Dear Sabbath home, once more we come, Hail-ing our
blooming a-new; Morn's gen-tle ray, gold-en and gay, Shines on the
fadeless and fair; Sav-iour and King, glad-ly we bring Praise for Thy

Ju-bi-lee this hap-py day; Eyes beaming brightly, hearts bounding
lil-y bells sparkling with dew; Beau-ty is call-ing, mu-sic is
precious love, Thy ten-der care; Gathered be-fore Thee, young hearts a-

light-ly, Now we sing our mer-ry, mer-ry lay: Dear Sabbath home,
fall-ing, Now a-gain earth wakes her joyful lay: Dear Sabbath home,
dore Thee, Sav-iour, hear, O hear our hap-py lay: Dear Sabbath home,

once more we come, Hail-ing our Ju-bi-lee, this hap-py day.

Copyright, 1885, by W. H. Doane.

No. 88. The Saviour is Waiting.

W. O. CUSHING.   ROBERT LOWRY.

1. The Sav-iour is wait-ing and call-ing, He bids us come in
2. He spread all His bounties be-fore them, He sought them wher-e'er
3. Have you ev - er thought of His mer - cy? He gra- cious - ly calls

to the feast; O come, all ye hun- gry and sad ones, There's
they might roam; With love trembling sweet in His mes-sage, He
you to - day; The feast of His love still is wait- ing; O

room for the worst and the least. }
ten - der-ly bade them come home. } Once they all made light of the
turn not, O turn not a - way. }

CHORUS.

sto- ry, And turned to their pleasure and sin; The proud and the care-

less de-spised Him, But the hum- ble and poor en - tered in.

Copyright, 1886, by Biglow & Main.

(89)

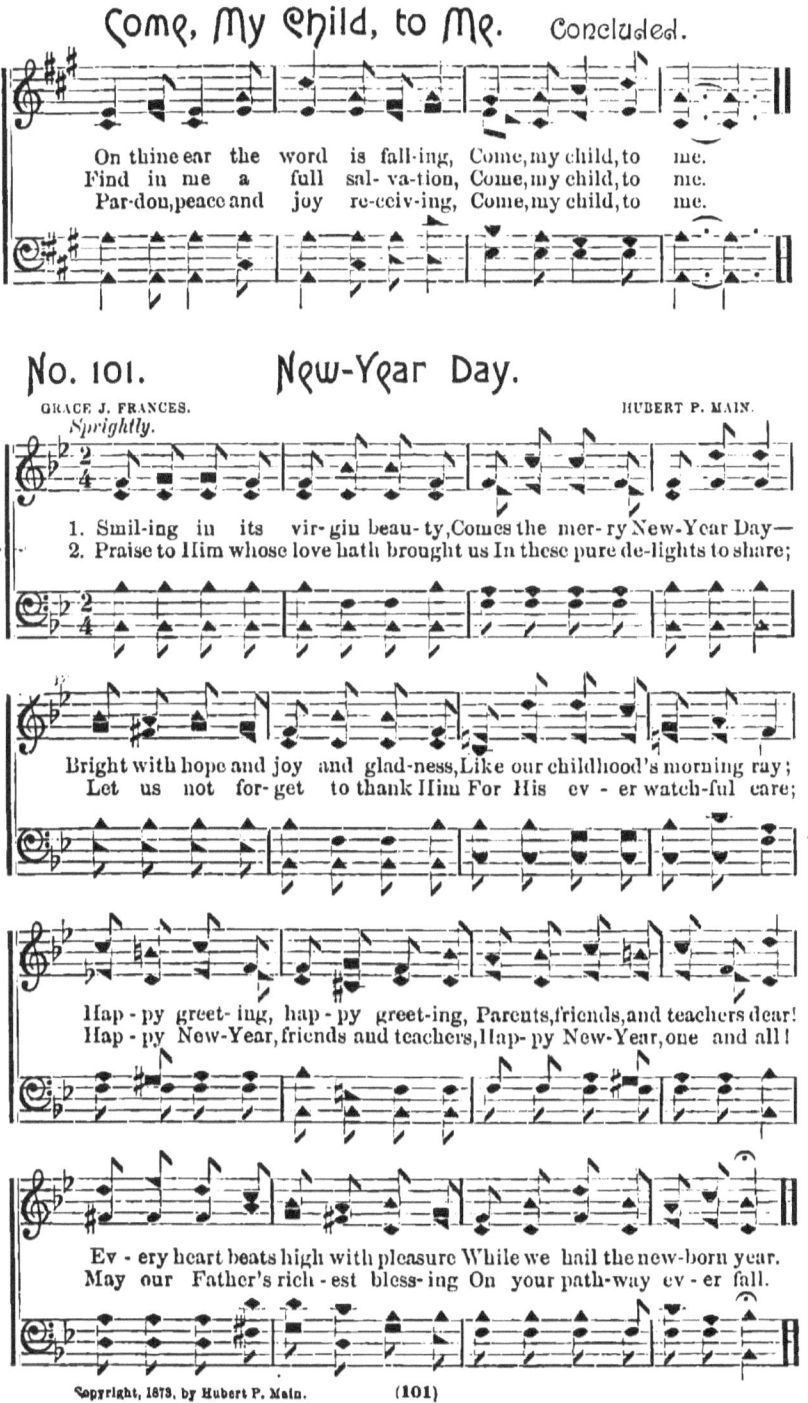

No. 106. Bless Our Souls Once More.

W. O. CUSHING.   ROBERT LOWRY.

1. There is no dew on the mountains of Zi-on, Dark are the paths where Thy glo-ry was known; We pray Thee, O Sav-iour, re-turn to Thy dwell-ing, O make our hearts Thine own......
2. There is no word on the lips of Thy peo-ple, Cold are the hearts that had loved Thee so long; And harps that a-woke to the prais-es of Je-sus Now wake no more in song......
3. Why should we sleep while the moments are fly-ing? Souls in their dark-ness and sin may be lost; How can we for-get they are liv-ing a-round us, Bought at so great a cost?.....

CHORUS.

Come, O come where Thy peo-ple are bend-ing, Come as once in the days of yore; Come, O come with Thy Spirit's re-turn-ing, Bless our

Copyright, 1866, by Biglow & Main.

Not a Stranger. Concluded.

But now I'm not a stran-ger, Je - sus is my Friend.
But now, but now

No. 121.   O The Rapture!

GRACE J. FRANCES.   HUBERT P. MAIN.

1. When we hear the dis-tant mur-mur Of the dark and swell-ing tide;
2. When we clasp the hand of Je - sus, And we hear His voice a - new;
3. When the ties of hallowed friendship Are u - nit - ed one by one,
4. Let us work and wait with patience, For the time is draw-ing nigh,

When we step a - cross the wa - ters, And have gained the oth - er side,—
When we think of all the tri - als That His love has brought us through,—
And we know that all our sor-rows And our mourning days are done,—
When our bless-ed Lord will call us To a home be - yond the sky.

CHORUS.   rit.

O the rapt-ure, ho - ly rapt-ure, When we press the gold-en shore,

tempo.   rit.

Sing-ing, Glo - ry! Hal - le - lu - jah! To the Lamb for - ev - er more.

Copyright, 1886, by Biglow & Main.

No. 123. Thy Promise Tells Me So.

FANNY J. CROSBY.   W. B. BRADBURY.

1. Dear Jesus, Thou wilt hear me, Thou art ev-er near me; Thy words of promise cheer me Where'er I go; Tho' young, I may believe Thee, Thy mer-cy will re-ceive me, And Thou wilt nev-er leave me—Thy prom-ise tells me so.
2. Dear Jesus, I a-dore Thee, Kind-ly watching o'er me; The way is bright be-fore me Where'er I go; Thy gracious throne ad-dress-ing, And all my sins con-fess-ing, A child may ask Thy bless-ing—Thy prom-ise tells me so.
3. Thy name sal-va-tion bring-ing, How my heart is sing-ing, While faith to Thee is cling-ing Where'er I go; Thou source of all my pleas-ure, Thy love I can-not meas-ure; Thou hast for me a treasure—Thy prom-ise tells me so.

Refrain.

Thou wilt pro-tect me, pro-tect me, pro-tect me; Thou wilt pro-tect me wher-e'er I go.

Copyright, 1866, by Biglow & Main.

No. 124. There's a Saviour on High.

WM. STEVENSON. ROBERT LOWRY.

1. There's a Sav-iour on high, And He bids me draw nigh; He has promised to an-swer my prayer; He will par-don my sin, Will re-new me with-in, And my heart for His dwell-ing pre-pare.
2. Long in sin I have lain, And have la-bored in vain From its fet-ters my spir-it to free; But no ef-fort of mine E'er its bands can un-twine, Or bring hope or de-liv-'rance to me.
3. When His fa-vor I know, There is noth-ing be-low That from Je-sus my soul can remove; When earth's conflicts are past, And there's vic-t'ry at last, He will bring me to man-sions a-bove.

CHORUS.

Then to Je-sus I'll go, For He loves me, I know, And no long-er His Spir-it I'll grieve; From my sins He'll re-lease, Give me

Copyright, 1886, by Biglow & Main. (122)

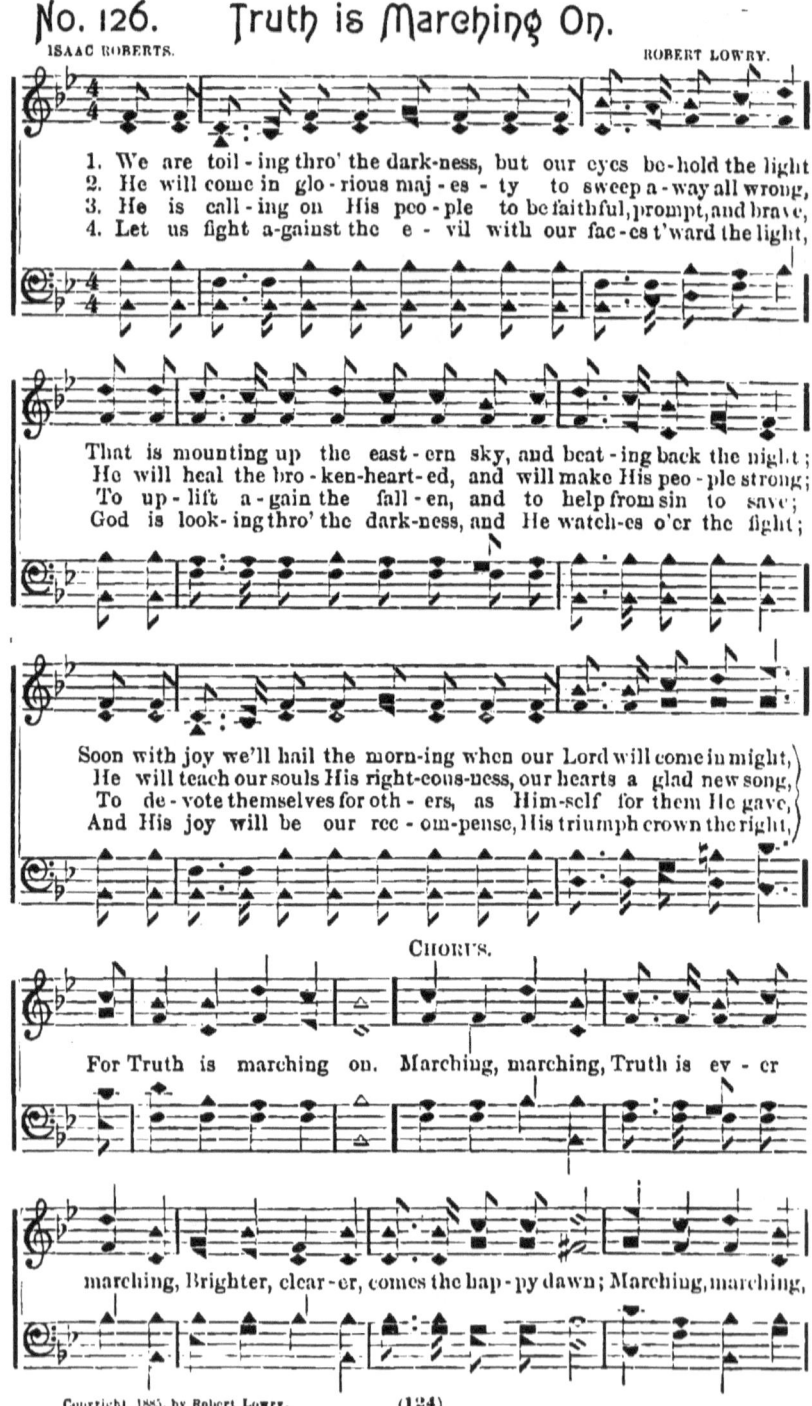

No. 128. Throng His Gates with Praise.

Mrs. CORA LINDEN.   W. H. DOANE.

1. To God who claims our high-est praise, Let ev-ery heart a song of tri-umph raise; Our faith leads on-ward to the tem-ple gates, Where Je-sus our Re-deem-er in glo-ry waits.
2. Our lives, our all, to Him we owe; With ea-ger joy we haste our love to show; Our love leads on-ward to the tem-ple gates, Where Je-sus our Re-deem-er so kind-ly waits.
3. The Lord is great, and yet we share The rich-es of His grace, His ten-der care; Our hope leads on-ward to the tem-ple gates, Where Je-sus our Re-deem-er His chil-dren waits.

REFRAIN.

We'll throng, we'll throng, We'll throng His gates with praise, We'll throng His gates with praise, throng His gates with ho-ly joy-ful praise; O hail the King of

Copyright, 1886, by Biglow & Main.

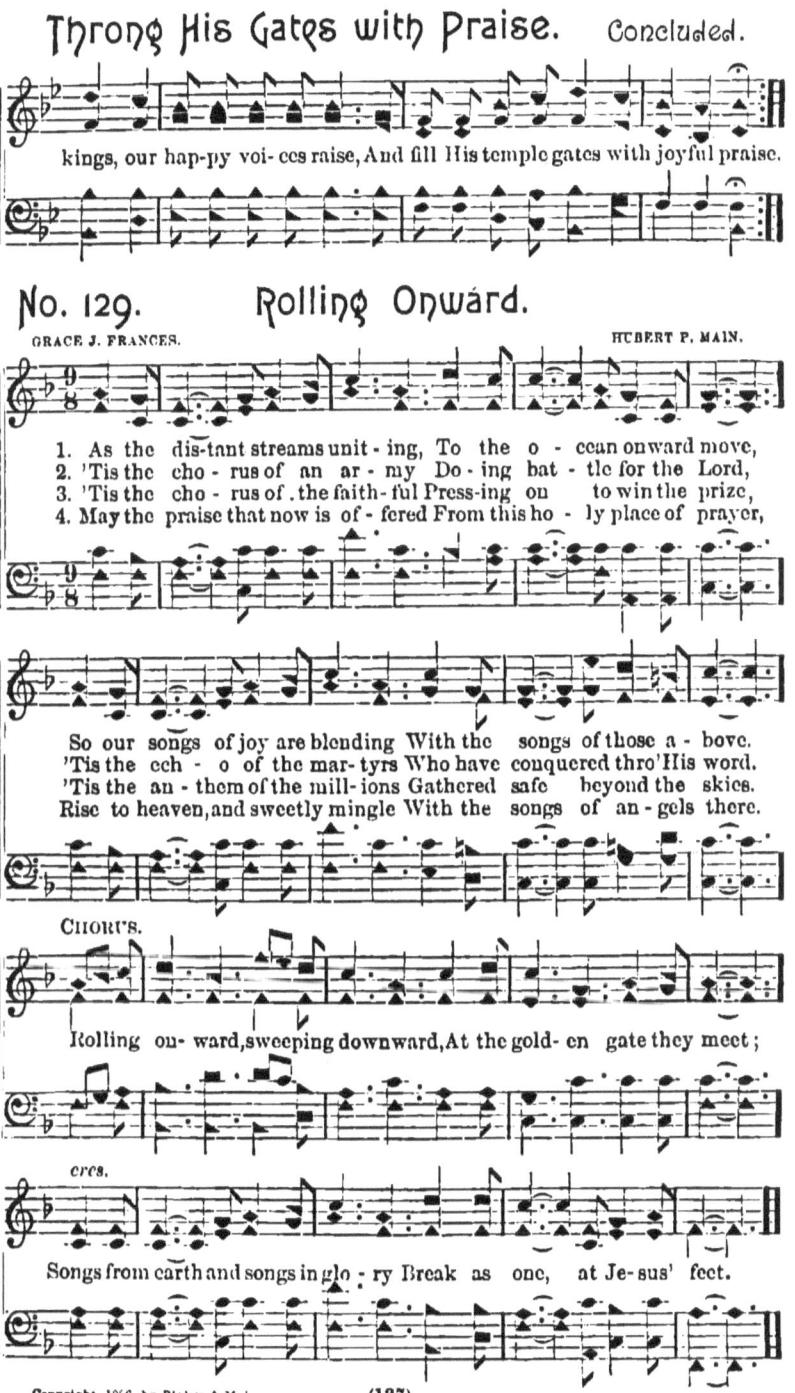

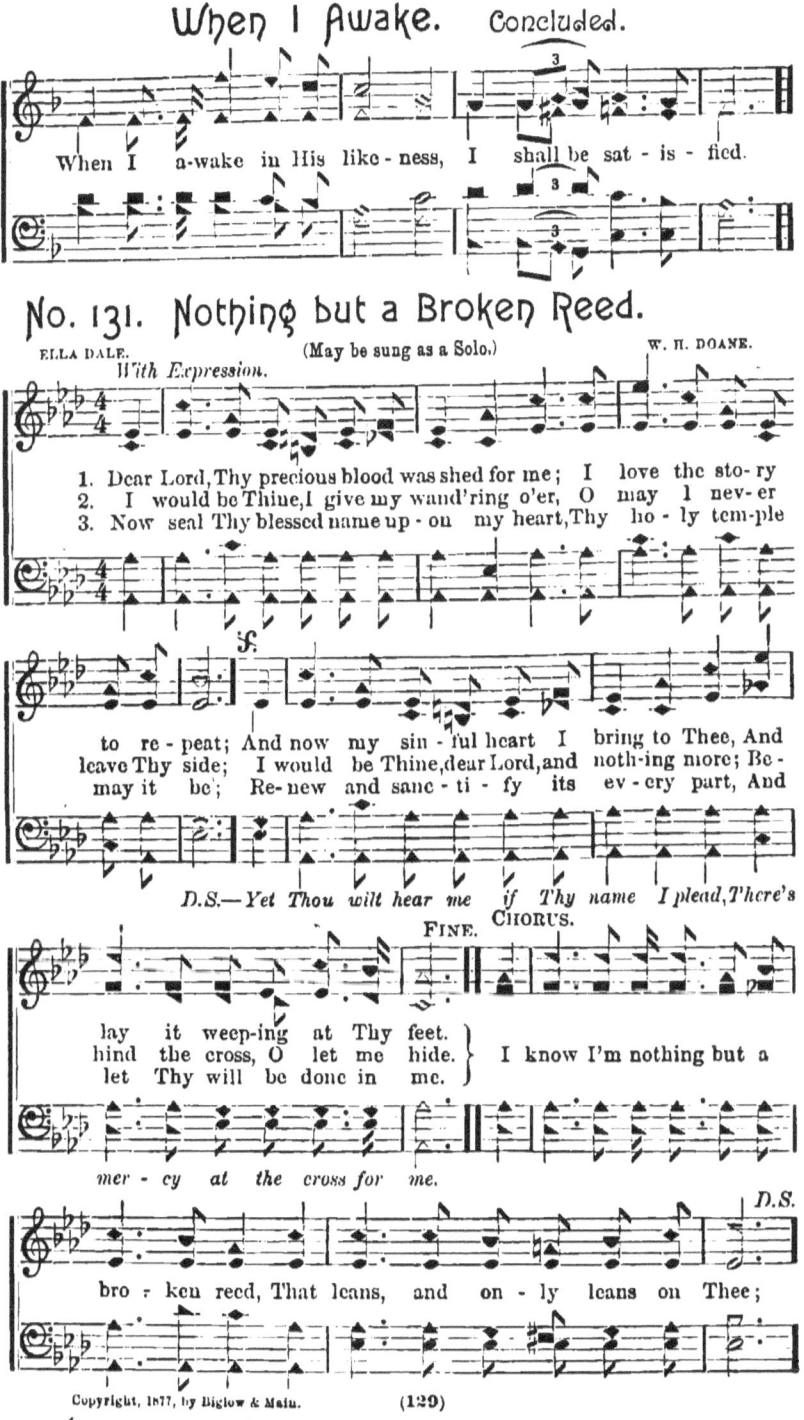

No. 140. Thro' the Gates of the City.

FANNY J. CROSBY. ROBERT LOWRY.

SOLO or CHORUS.

1. Thro' the gates of the cit-y they are pass-ing, one by one,
   The re-deemed who have conquered, and whose lives have just be-gun;
   For the Lord their Redeem-er at the shin-ing port-als stands,
   And ap-points them their mansions in the house not made with hands.

2. Thro' the gates of the cit-y they have en-tered, one by one,
   They who toiled for the Mas-ter, and whose har-vest work is done;
   They who sowed to the spir-it, and have reaped a rich re-ward,
   Come with sheaves bright and golden, sing-ing glo-ry to the Lord.

3. When the night falls up-on us, and our vine-yard work is done,
   Thro' the gates of the cit-y may we en-ter, one by one;
   May the Lord keep us faith-ful till the storms of life are past,
   That we lose not the glo-ry when the jour-ney ends at last.

CHORUS.

From the soul's hap-py rest-ing, Nev-er—
From the soul's hap-py rest-ing, from the soul's hap-py rest-ing, Nev-er—

Copyright, 1886, by Biglow & Main. (138)

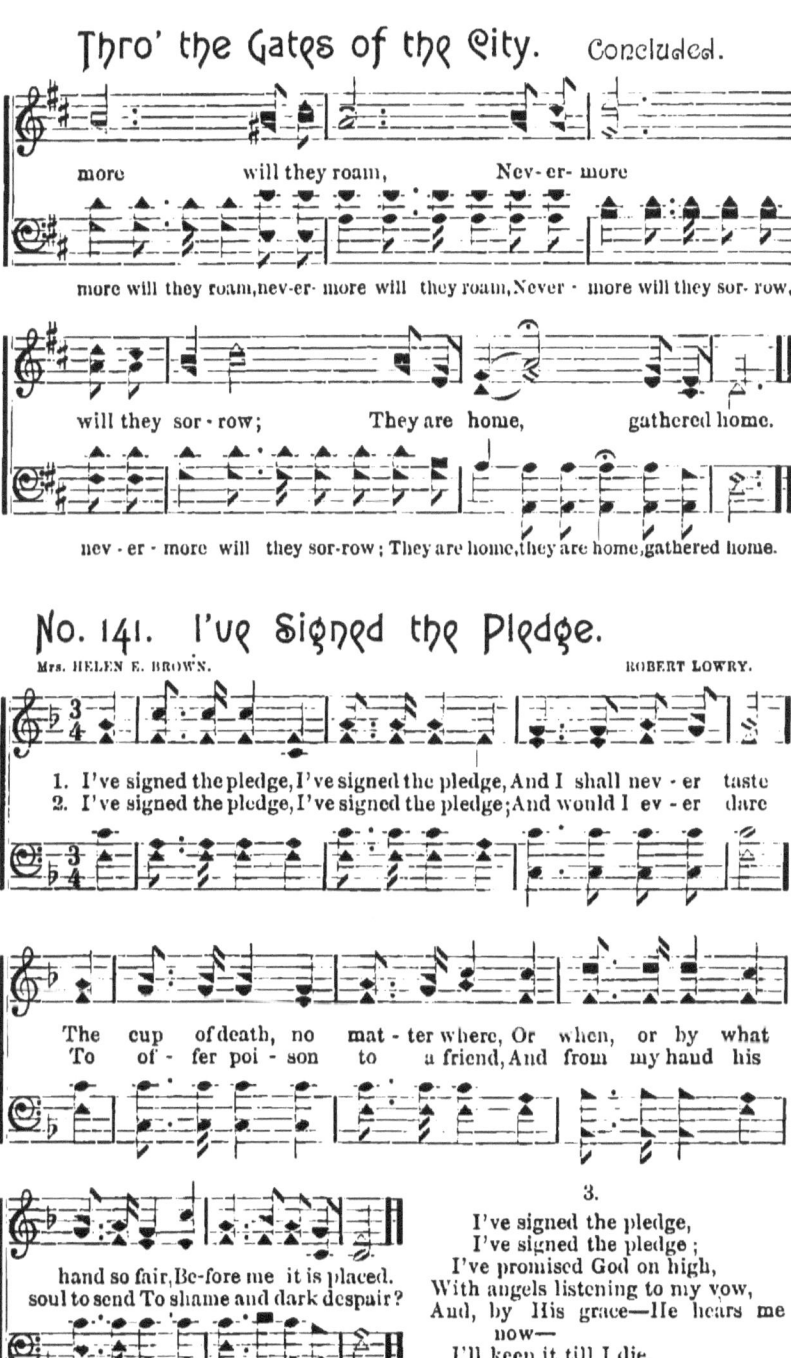

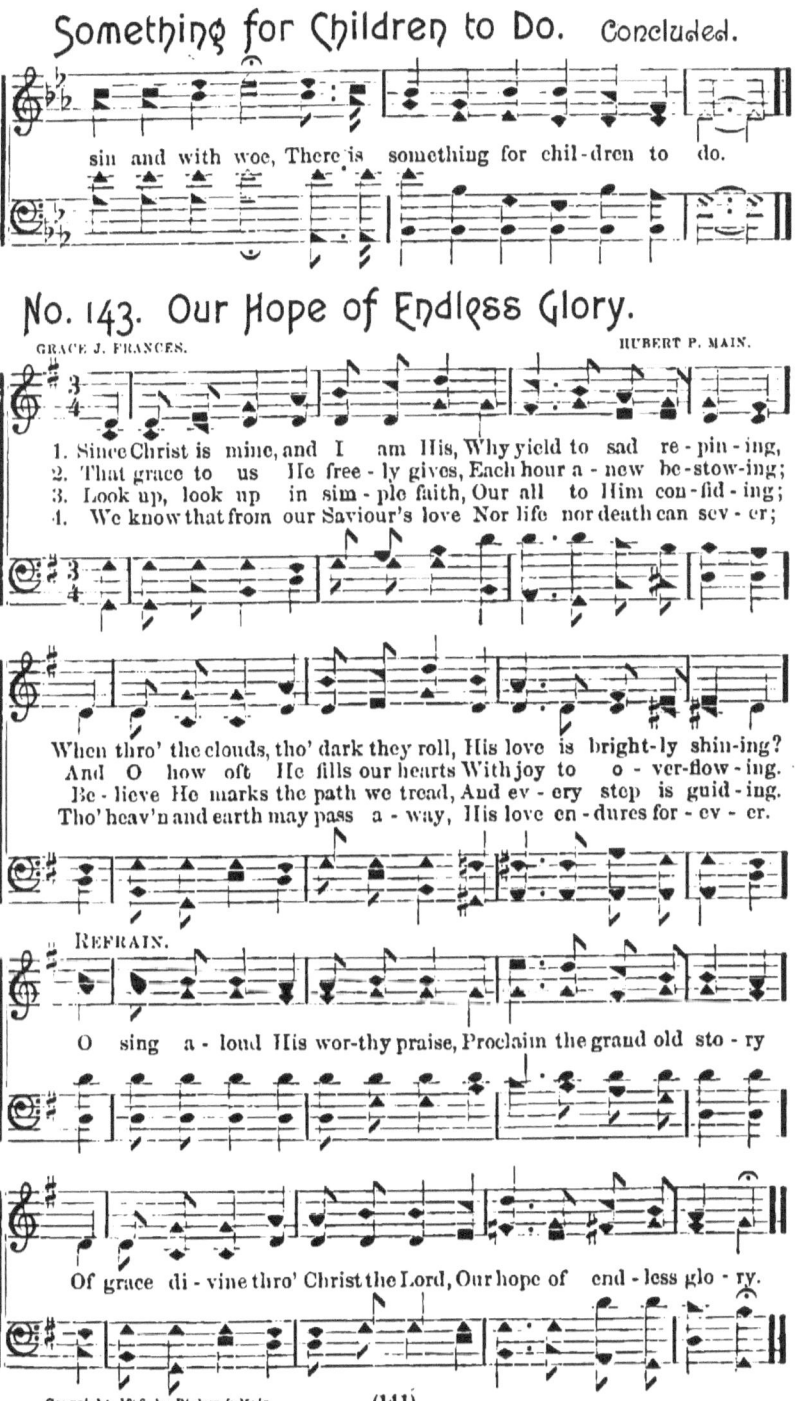

The Anchored Soul. Concluded.

safe ev-er-more, ev-er-more, But in Je-sus I'm safe ev-er-more.

No. 147. Learn of Jesus.

GRACE J. FRANCES.   HUBERT P. MAIN.

1. Haste a-way, O haste a-way, Come and learn of Je-sus;
2. He is just the friend we need, None can save but Je-sus;
3. Once He laid His crown a-side, O the love of Je-sus!
4. Come and join us while we sing, Glo-ry be to Je-sus;

Bright with joy our home to-day, Come and learn of Je-sus.
Come and learn His name to plead, None can save but Je-sus.
On the cross for us He died, O the love of Je-sus!
Let the joy-ful cho-rus ring, Glo-ry be to Je-sus.

CHORUS.

Hear the voice that speaks to all, Now His words like mu-sic fall;

In His heart there's room for all, Come and learn of Je-sus.

Copyright, 1886, by Biglow & Main.

No. 153. With an Earnest Will.

FANNY J. CROSBY.   W. H. DOANE.

1. Let us take our place in the field of grace, To the work with ardor bend-ing, And the right pur-sue with a pur-pose true, On the Saviour a-lone de-pend-ing; With an earnest will, pressing onward still, Our Redeem-er watch-ing o'er us, We shall rest ere long in the land of song, With the faith-ful gone be-fore us.
2. With an ear-nest will, pressing on-ward still, Let us work and never wea-ry, For the Lord is near, and the heart will cheer Tho' the sky may be sometimes dreary; While the fields are bright, and the days are light, And the har-vest call is sound-ing, Let us bear our part with a trust-ing heart, And a song of joy re-sound-ing;
3. Let our faith a-bound, let us all be found In the work of love and du-ty, Till the shad-ows fall, and we hear the call To a mansion of fade-less beau-ty; If we work and pray in the good old way, To the Sav-iour close-ly keep-ing, When our work is done, and our crown is won, There will be a glo-rious reap-ing.

D.S.—take our place in the field of grace, &c.

Copyright, 1886, by Biglow & Main.

All Around is Bright and Fair. Concluded.

REFRAIN.

Come, O come,...... this cheer-ful, hap-py day;
O come,
Come, O come,...... to Sun-day School a - way.
O come,

No. 157.   Jesus, My Lord.

FANNY J. VAN ALSTYNE.   T. J. COOK.

1. What have I done for Thee, Je-sus, my Lord? Yet dost Thou
2. What have I done for Thee, Je-sus, my Lord? Yet hast Thou
3. What have I done for Thee, Je-sus, my Lord? Yet hast Thou

care for me, Je-sus, my Lord! When I was far a-stray, Gen-tly I
bled for me, Je-sus, my Lord! O my un-grateful heart! Cleanse it in
died for me, Je-sus, my Lord! O how the crimson tide Streams from Thy

heard Thee say, I am the Liv-ing Way, I am the Lord.
ev-ery part; Thou my sal-va-tion art, Je-sus, my Lord.
wound-ed side! Je-sus, the cru-ci-fied, Je-sus, my Lord.

Copyright, 1886, by Biglow & Main.

Hymns.

No. 160. Tune, CORONATION.
1 All hail the power of Jesus' name!
    Let angels prostrate fall;
Bring forth the royal diadem,
    And crown Him Lord of all.

2 Let every kindred, every tribe,
    On this terrestrial ball,
To Him all majesty ascribe,
    And crown Him Lord of all.

3 O that with yonder sacred throng,
    We at His feet may fall;
We'll join the everlasting song,
    And crown Him Lord of all.

No. 161. Tune, DENNIS.
1 Blest be the tie that binds
    Our hearts in Christian love;
The fellowship of kindred minds
    Is like to that above.

2 Before our Father's throne
    We pour our ardent prayers;
Our fears, our hopes, our aims, are one,
    Our comforts and our cares.

3 This glorious hope revives
    Our courage by the way;
While each in expectation lives,
    And longs to see the day.

No. 162. Tune, TOPLADY.
1 Rock of Ages, cleft for me,
    Let me hide myself in Thee;
Let the water and the blood,
    From Thy wounded side which flowed,
Be of sin a double cure,
    Save from wrath and make me pure.

2 Could my tears forever flow,
    Could my zeal no languor know—
This for sin could not atone;
    Thou must save, and Thou alone;
In my hand no price I bring,
    Simply to Thy cross I cling.

No. 163. Tune, BEAUTIFUL RIVER.
1 Shall we gather at the river
    Where bright angel feet have trod;
With its crystal tide forever
    Flowing from the throne of God?

CHO.—Yes, we'll gather at the river,
    The beautiful, the beautiful river—
Gather with the saints at the river
    That flows from the throne of God.

2 Soon we'll reach the shining river,
    Soon our pilgrimage will cease;
Soon our happy hearts will quiver
    With the melody of peace.
        CHO.—Yes, we'll gather, &c.

No. 164. Tune, BROWN.
1 I love to steal awhile away
    From every cumbering care,
And spend the hours of setting day
    In humble, grateful prayer.

2 I love to think on mercies past,
    And future good implore,—
And all my cares and sorrows cast
    On Him whom I adore.

No. 165. Tune, SWEET HOUR.
1 Sweet hour of prayer! sweet hour of
        prayer!
That calls me from a world of care,
And bids me at my Father's throne
Make all my wants and wishes known;
In seasons of distress and grief,
My soul has often found relief,
And oft escaped the tempter's snare,
By thy return, sweet hour of prayer.

2 Sweet hour of prayer! sweet hour of
        prayer!
May I thy consolation share,
Till, from Mount Pisgah's lofty height,
I view my home, and take my flight;
This robe of flesh I'll drop, and rise
To seize the everlasting prize;
And shout, while passing through the air,
Farewell, farewell, sweet hour of prayer!

No. 66. Tune, MARTYN.
1 Jesus, lover of my soul,
    Let me to Thy bosom fly,
While the billows near me roll,
    While the tempest still is high;
Hide me, O my Saviour, hide,
    Till the storm of life be past;
Safe into the haven guide;
    O receive my soul at last.

2 Thou, O Christ, art all I want,
    More than all in Thee I find;
Raise the fallen, cheer the faint,
    Heal the sick, and lead the blind;
Just and holy is Thy name,
    I am all unrighteousness;
Vile and full of sin I am—
    Thou art full of truth and grace.

No. 167. Tune, PRECIOUS NAME.
1 Take the name of Jesus with you,
    Child of sorrow and of woe—
It will joy and comfort give you,
    Take it, then, where'er you go.

CHO. ‖: Precious name, O how sweet,
    Hope of earth and joy of heaven. :‖

2 Take the name of Jesus ever,
    As a shield from every snare;
If temptations round you gather,
    Breathe that Holy Name in prayer.

No. 168. Tune, WEBB.
1 The morning light is breaking,
    The darkness disappears;
The sons of earth are waking
    To penitential tears;
Each breeze that sweeps the ocean
    Brings tidings from afar,
Of nations in commotion,
    Prepared for Zion's war.

2 Rich dews of grace come o'er us,
    In many a gentle shower,
And brighter scenes before us
    Are opening every hour;
Each cry to heaven going
    Abundant answer brings,
And heavenly gales are blowing
    With peace upon their wings.

Index of Subjects.

---o---

This Index is of a very general character. A careful examination of the book will enable the Leader to select many hymns for special use which are not given in minute analysis of subjects. It is intended that suitable hymns shall be found for any occasion likely to arise in the work of the Sunday School. The Numbers refer to the *hymns*, not the pages.

ACTIVITY—5, 6, 19, 29, 33, 41, 49, 52, 61, 63, 64, 68, 69, 80, 110, 115, 126, 132, 134, 142, 150, 153, 156.

ANNIVERSARIES—28, 84, 101.

BIBLE—95.

CHRIST: BIRTH—40, 44, 70, 85.
    RESURRECTION—43, 55, 56, 73, 86.
    COMING—6, 12, 126.

CLOSING—22, 25, 62.

DEPENDENCE—9, 10, 14, 15, 24, 75, 114, 118, 135, 136.

FAITH—3, 4, 14, 23, 26, 30, 31, 34, 36, 42, 51, 53, 57, 61, 97, 99, 104, 111, 120, 123, 127, 145, 146, 154, 161, 166, 167.

HEAVEN—16, 17, 27, 32, 48, 67, 71, 72, 74, 79, 90, 91, 105, 121, 122, 125, 130, 137, 140, 144, 148, 159, 163.

HOLY SPIRIT—18, 92, 112, 152.

INVITATION—2, 7, 35, 38, 39, 54, 56, 58, 81, 88, 89, 100, 133, 147, 155.

MISSIONS—151, 168.

NEW YEAR—101.

OPENING—47, 65, 77, 78, 87, 127.

PRAISE—1, 2, 11, 20, 21, 46, 50, 55, 59, 60, 70, 73, 84, 96, 109, 117, 128, 129, 143, 158, 160.

PRAYER—10, 83, 87, 119, 150, 164, 165.

PRIMARY SONGS—8, 37, 107, 116, 136.

REPENTANCE—34, 53, 66, 103, 106, 113, 124, 131, 138, 139, 150, 157.

SALVATION—3, 13, 31, 45, 60, 76, 82, 93, 94, 102, 108, 162.

SUNDAY SCHOOL—11, 25, 47, 50, 156.

TEMPERANCE—49, 126, 138, 141.

INDEX.

Titles in SMALL CAPS.—First Lines in Roman.

	NO.
A FEW MORE MARCHINGS WEARY	67
ALL AROUND IS BRIGHT AND FAIR	156
ALL FOR THE BEST	23
ALL HAIL, BLESSED MORNING	43
All hail the power of Jesus' name	160
ALL MY LIFE LONG	51
A LOVING FRIEND	99
ALTOGETHER LOVELY	96
"Arise, young man, arise!"	56
As I sought, with weary flitting	108
A song, a song of joy	60
As the distant streams	129
AT THE LOVELY PALACE GATE	71
At the sounding of the trumpet	17
AWAKE, O VOICE OF MUSIC	55
BEAUTIFUL EDEN	122
BENEDICTION	22
BEYOND THIS VALE	12
BLESSED BIBLE	95
Blessed Hope of my salvation	135
BLESSED KING OF JUDAH	21
BLESSED SABBATH	8
BLESS OUR SOULS ONCE MORE	106
Blest be the tie that binds	161
BRIGHT HOME ABOVE	137
BRINGING IN THE SHEAVES	33
BY THE BLOOD OF THE LAMB	31
By the cross of Christ I linger	3
CHARGE and encourage them	63
CLEANSED AND REDEEMED	76
Cleansed in the blood that was shed	76
CLING TO THE SAVIOUR	111
COME AGAIN	25
COME AT THE CALL	7
COME, HOLY SPIRIT	18
Come, Holy Spirit, Light Divine	18
COME, LEARN OF THE MEEK AND	38
COME, MY CHILD, TO ME	100
COME UNTO ME	97
Come, ye saints! look here and wonder	86
COMING HOME TO-NIGHT	53
CRY FOR HELP	151
DAILY, HOURLY, LEAD ME	14
Dear Jesus, Thou wilt hear me	123
Dear Lord, Thy precious blood	131
Dear Saviour, let Thy watchful eye	75

	NO.
EARLY SEEKING	103
Early will I wake, and heed	103
EVER FAITHFUL	104
EVER WITH THE LORD	148
EVERY DAY FOR JESUS	116
FOLLOW THE STANDARD	63
FULL ATONEMENT	82
GLORY, GLORY!	59
Glory, glory, glory!	78
GLORY IN THE HIGHEST	44
GOD BE WITH YOU	62
GO LEAD THEM TO-DAY	80
Good news, good news	40
GREAT IS THE LORD	78
HAIL HIM	11
Happy faces turning now	64
Hark, hark again, angelic voices	44
Hark, hark the song, gliding along	84
Hark, 'tis the gospel trumpet	41
Hark that cry of deep and earnest	151
Have you spent a pleasant day?	25
Haste away, O haste away	147
HAVEN, BRIGHT HAVEN	105
HEARKEN, YE SOLDIERS	68
Hear the Saviour gently calling	100
HEAVEN IS MINE	32
HE IS RISEN TO-DAY	86
HE PAID THE PRICE	60
HIDE ME	24
Hide me, O my Saviour, hide me	24
HOLD UP THE CROSS	3
Holy Ghost, in sovereign power	152
HOLY SPIRIT, NOW DESCEND	112
HOMES FOR THE CHILDREN	144
HOW LONG?	155
How many sheep are straying	134
I AM Jesus' little, little friend	37
I'm resting so sweetly in Jesus	146
I AM SAVED BY THE BLOOD	94
I have a royal message	89
I have laid my all, dear Saviour	154
I'VE SIGNED THE PLEDGE	141
I KNOW THERE'S A REST	16
I love to steal awhile away	164

(158)

INDEX.

Title	NO.
In our duty, Lord, to Thee	104
Is my name written there?	71
It is all for the best	23
It is good to be here	127
I'll praise Him while I live	109
I'll take Thy Name where'er I go	46
Jesus, I am coming	113
Jesus, let me come to Thee	113
Jesus, lover of my soul	166
Jesus loves me too	37
Jesus, my Lord	157
Joy to all	70
Joy, joy to all, O happy, happy	70
Just a little	118
Just a little love, Lord	118
Just one way	81
Keep looking up, keep looking up	42
Keep Thou me	135
Knocking at the door	39
Land above	27
Lead me to Jesus	136
Learn of Jesus	147
Let the sound go forth	40
Let us take our place	153
Life is full of evil, brother	7
Light immortal, shine	92
Light of light	77
List, 'tis the Saviour calling	133
Little Eyes	107
Living water	108
Looking up	42
Look to the precious Jesus	30
Lord, answer our prayer	10
Lord, I bow at Thy throne	150
Lord, I care not for riches	71
Loving hearts we bring	137
Loving Redeemer, behold us to-day	97
Loving Saviour, lead me	14
Marching in the sunlight	64
Mine be a hope that is changeless	4
My soul was long a stranger	120
My trust is in Jesus alone	26
Near to the Saviour, O come	87
News of redemption thro' Christ	102
New Year Day	101
No other name but Jesus	109
Not a stranger	120
Not far from the Kingdom	58
Nothing but a broken reed	131
Now and forever	114
O can it be, O can it be	45
O hear the trump of joy	85
O how bright, cheerfully bright	11
O I cannot take it in	130
O Lord, my heart is Thine	57

Title	NO.
O Mother dear, Jerusalem	159
O my Redeemer, while Thy throne	114
Once again	65
Only a little way	91
Only one foundation	4
Only one name	1
On, press on	115
O pity the erring	80
O precious Redeemer, we come	10
O remember there's a work	61
O Saviour, I have promised	15
O sweet are the moments	22
O the rapture	121
O there is none like the blessed King	21
O they need not depart	132
O Thou that hearest prayer	119
Our hope of endless glory	143
Our joyful notes we gladly raise	117
Our jubilee song	81
Our song of jubilee	28
O what a Saviour is mine	36
O what blessed words are these	148
Peaceful and beautiful haven	105
"Perfect." O Lord!	9
Pity one another	138
Precious Hope	13
Precious Invitation	133
Precious is the hope	13
Promptly on time	47
Purchased for me	102
Rock of Ages, cleft for me	162
Rolling Onward	129
Saved by His blood	93
Save, save one	52
Saviour, I come to Thee	66
Saviour, I have promised	15
Saviour, pass not by	31
Seek salvation to-day	35
Send the victory	5
Shall we gather at the river	163
Shall we meet one another?	90
Since Christ is mine, and I am His	143
Sing of the Bright Forever	72
Sing, O sing of the Bright Forever	72
Smiling in its virgin beauty	101
Soldiers of the Lord	49
Something for children to do	142
Souls are perishing before thee	52
Sowing in the morning	33
Stand by the right	98
Strike your golden lyres	48
Sweet are the bells	73
Sweet hour of prayer!	165
Sweet moments	20
Take the name of Jesus with you	167
Thanks to God we give	95
The anchored soul	146
The children are coming, united	50
The everlasting arms	154

(159)

INDEX.

	NO.
The grace of our Lord Jesus Christ...	22
THE HOUR OF WORSHIP.	152
THE HUMBLE HEART.	75
THE LOST SHEEP.	134
The morning light is breaking	168
There's a land above.	27
There is a land where shines the light	79
THERE'S A SAVIOUR ON HIGH	121
There is just one way for us all.	81
There is no dew on the mountains.	106
There is only one Name.	1
There is something on earth.	142
There is work to do for Jesus.	110
THE ROYAL MESSAGE.	89
The Saviour called so lovingly	93
THE SAVIOUR IS WAITING.	88
THE SOUL'S BRIGHT LAND ABOVE.	79
THE SUNDAY SCHOOL ARMY	50
THE SWEETEST NAME.	46
The welcome news my soul makes glad	32
THEY NEED NOT DEPART.	132
THOU CAREST FOR ME.	145
Tho' all men forsake Him.	29
Though surrounded by foes.	31
THRONE OF ETERNAL LOVE	149
THRONG His GATES WITH PRAISE.	128
THRO' THE GATES OF THE CITY	140
THY PROMISE TELLS ME SO.	123
'Tis only a little way.	91
To God who claims our highest praise	128
TRAVELING HOMEWARD.	125
TRUTH IS MARCHING ON	126
UNTO THE LORD.	117
UP AND WORK.	69
Up with the morning	115
Vesper bells are ringing.	96

	NO.
WAIT AT HIS THRONE.	87
WAIT ON THE LORD.	2
WAS IT FOR ME?.	45
WATCH AND PRAY.	83
We are hoping on.	5
We are ransomed by a King	74
We are soldiers of the Lord.	49
We are toiling thro' the darkness.	126
We come, our Redeemer.	158
WE MUST BE TRUE.	29
We never shall be happy.	35
WE PRAISE THEE.	158
We should think how we all feel.	138
We sing our song of Jubilee.	28
WHAT A GATHERING THAT WILL BE.	17
What have I done for Thee	157
WHAT MERCY!.	26
WHEN I AWAKE.	130
WHEN SHALL I COME TO JESUS?.	139
When the blush of morning light.	83
When we hear the distant murmur.	121
WHILE THE GOLDEN SCEPTRE WAITS.	54
While we bow in Thy name	127
WHO'LL BE SOWING?.	19
WITH AN EARNEST WILL.	153
WITH A PERSEVERING FAITH.	61
Wonderful, wonderful Saviour.	145
WORK, FOR THE DAY IS COMING.	6
Working for the Master.	98
WORK TO DO FOR JESUS.	110
YES, I'm coming home to Jesus.	53
YOUNG MAN, ARISE.	56
ZION'S HAPPY SOLDIERS.	41

www.ingramcontent.com/pod-product-compliance
Lightning Source LLC
Chambersburg PA
CBHW030316170426
43202CB00009B/1030